WORLD WAR II

WORLD
WAR II

by Philip Clark

Illustrated by Jim Dugdale
and Gerald Witcomb

GRANADA PUBLISHING

Published by Granada 1984
Granada Publishing Limited
8 Grafton Street, London W1X 3LA

Copyright © Granada Publishing 1984

British Library Cataloguing in Publication Data
Clark, Philip
  World War II. – (Granada guides)
  1. World War, 1939–1945 – Juvenile literature
  I. Title
  940.53   D743.7

ISBN 0-246-12166-1

Printed in Great Britain by
Collins, Glasgow

Contents

Background to the War

The Second World War was really two separate conflicts. One of these was the war against Germany and her allies. The other was the war against Japan, for Germany and Japan were too far apart to help each other significantly.

The beginnings of the war with Germany can be traced back at least as far as the end of World War I. In 1919 a defeated Germany had no choice except to sign the Treaty of Versailles. There was a desire to 'make Germany pay for the war', and the terms of the treaty were harsh.

The terms of the Treaty of Versailles included the payment by Germany of vast 'reparations', or war debts. Alsace-Lorraine was handed back to France, and the victorious Allies occupied the Rhineland. The French Marshal Foch commented: 'This is not peace. It is an armistice for twenty years.'

Germany's failure to pay the reparations resulted in the occupation of the Ruhr, her great industrial centre, by French and Belgian troops in 1923. This occupation caused great resentment in Germany. The reparations were first scaled down, and finally cancelled altogether. Two years later, at Locarno, Britain, France, Germany and Italy signed a treaty not to wage war on each other.

Allied Powers – red
Axis Powers – blue
Neutral Countries – yellow

● Moscow

USSR

BLACK SEA

BULGARIA

TURKEY

The map shows the two sides at the outbreak of World War II. Germany had already occupied Austria and Czechoslovakia. This gave her a long border across which to attack Poland – the event that started the war.

At this time East Prussia was a German state separated from the rest of Germany by the 'Polish Corridor', which gave Poland access to the Baltic Sea.

The alliance between Germany and Italy, called the Axis, was joined by more and more countries as Europe fell under German dominance. Russia remained neutral at first because she had an agreement with Germany, but when Hitler broke this pact in 1941 and invaded her, she joined the Allies.

The Rise of Adolf Hitler

The leader of Germany throughout the war was Adolf Hitler. The son of an Austrian customs official, Hitler spent his youth in poverty in Vienna. He served as a corporal in the German army during World War I, and received the Iron Cross for bravery. After the war Hitler became leader of the National Socialist (Nazi) Party.

Following the Great Depression of 1929, Germany suffered badly from unemployment. Many of the unemployed joined the Nazis, which eventually became the largest political party. In 1933 Hitler became chancellor (prime minister) of Germany.

Hitler, in the uniform of the SA (his private army) grasps a Nazi flag. In 1923 he failed in an attempt to seize power, and spent nine months in prison.

8

Hitler swiftly silenced his opponents. Jews were persecuted, and many fled abroad. Hitler's dream was the establishment of a 'Greater Germany'. This involved the expansion of Germany eastward through Poland into Russia. Hitler knew he would have to take this land by force, and he built up Germany's armed forces. Despite warnings from Winston Churchill and others, Britain failed to keep pace with this escalation.

In 1936 German troops marched into the Rhineland. The British and French did nothing to stop them. The Spanish Civil War broke out in the same year and Hitler's forces gained valuable experience helping the Nationalists fight the Republicans.

Below left: The Italian dictator Benito Mussolini.
Below right: Neville Chamberlain, the British prime minister, believed that the Munich Agreement meant 'Peace in our time'.

The Outbreak of War

Encouraged by the success of his Rhineland gamble, Hitler's next move was to incorporate Austria into the German Reich (State). In March 1938 the German army crossed the Austrian border without

The speed and success of the German invasion of Poland surprised even Hitler. The Germans used Stuka dive-bombers to paralyse Polish resistance and clear a path for the tanks.

opposition. Hitler's aims were quickly achieved despite a large number of tank breakdowns.

Hitler's sights were now on Czechoslovakia. Mussolini, the Italian dictator, suggested a four-power conference between Britain, France, Germany and Italy. In September 1938 the various leaders met in Munich. Neville Chamberlain, the British prime minister, returned home afterwards happy in the belief that they had ensured 'Peace in our time'.

The Munich Agreement stated that Hitler could take over the German-speaking part of Czechoslovakia: he promptly went on to take over the whole country. The following year, Hitler signed the 'Pact of Steel' with Mussolini. Next he made a secret agreement with the Russians, which provided for the division of Poland between Russia and Germany. In the meantime Britain had offered to come to the aid of the Poles if Poland should be invaded.

The German army invaded Poland on 1 September 1939. On 3 September Britain and France declared war on Germany. The Poles fought bravely, but their forces were hopelessly out of date. The Germans made use of a new technique which they called *Blitzkrieg* (lightning war). This involved attacking with a combination of dive-bombers and tanks. Within a month Polish resistance had crumbled. The Russians quickly moved in to claim their share.

The Phoney War

During the fighting in Poland, the French army had advanced cautiously into Germany. When Poland fell, the French retreated behind their defensive Maginot Line. A small British Expeditionary Force was sent to France, but there was no fighting on the Western Front during the winter of 1939–1940. This period is known as the 'phoney war'.

Hitler decided that he needed to deliver a swift knock-out blow to France before invading Russia. His generals dusted off the 1914 Schlieffen invasion plan in which the Germans had laid out their successful first attack on France in World War I. But through an air accident, these plans fell into the hands of the Allies. The Schlieffen Plan was replaced by the Manstein Plan, which involved a powerful tank attack through Belgium.

The small but well-trained Finnish army proved, man for man, more than a match for the Russians during the Winter War.

German troops enter Oslo, the capital of Norway, by bicycle. Oslo was captured by airborne paratroops.

The War in the North

On 30 November 1939 Russia invaded Finland. The tiny Finnish army fought back fiercely, and managed to hold up the Russian advance until the following February. Finally, however, the Finns were over-whelmed by sheer weight of numbers.

Meanwhile, Hitler was becoming worried about the possibility of Allied landings in Scandinavia. So, on 9 April 1940, the Germans invaded Norway and Denmark. Allied troops were landed in Norway, but they proved no match for the Germans and had to be evacuated. This episode led to fierce criticism of the British government. Chamberlain resigned as prime minister, and was replaced by Winston Churchill.

The Road to Dunkirk

On 10 May 1940 the German army invaded Belgium, the Netherlands and Luxembourg. At this time the Allied troops actually outnumbered the Germans, but the defenders were stunned by the speed of the attack and the screaming of the Stuka dive-bombers. The Belgian fort of Eben Emael was captured by a small force of paratroops who landed on top of it.

Soon afterwards German tanks broke out of the forest of the Ardennes. This had previously been considered by the French to be 'impassable'. By 20 May the French army was in full retreat. The British succeeded briefly in holding up the German advance with a handful of tanks. They were soon forced, however, to retreat towards the Channel coast.

At this point Hitler gave his fateful order to halt the German tanks. It was undoubtedly this order that enabled Britain to get her troops home and continue the war. Various reasons have been given for Hitler's decision. It may be that he wished to preserve his tanks and leave it to his air force to finish off the British. Another possibility is that he wished to spare Britain the shame of utter defeat, in the hope that he could make peace.

At all events Hitler's order enabled almost the entire British army to escape from Dunkirk, with the help of the Royal Navy and an armada of small boats.

Nearly 340,000 men of the British army were evacuated at Dunkirk, but most of their equipment had to be abandoned.

The Fall of France

While the British army was being evacuated from Dunkirk, the French were regrouping on the rivers Somme and Aisne. But by this time many of the French troops had lost confidence, and many others had been captured.

The Germans renewed their attack on 5 June. After two days of fierce fighting, they broke through the French line. On the 10th the Italians under Mussolini, who had been waiting until German victory was certain, also declared war on France. On the 14th German troops entered Paris.

The armistice was signed on 22 June – in the same railway carriage in Compiègne that had been used for the German surrender in 1918. Northern France was to come under German occupation. Unoccupied France was to have a pro-German government, which made its headquarters in the town of Vichy. However, a French general, Charles de Gaulle, flew to London, where he organized continued French resistance to the Germans. (Many years later, de Gaulle was to become president of France).

Now, of all the countries that had been opposed to Hitler, only Britain remained undefeated, and her army had lost most of its equipment at Dunkirk. In those dark days Churchill inspired the British people with his famous speeches: '. . . we shall defend our island, whatever the cost may be. We shall fight on the beaches, we shall fight on the landing-grounds, we shall fight in the fields and in the streets, we shall fight in the hills; we shall never surrender . . .'

Right: German troops taking part in the Paris victory parade march past the Arc de Triomphe (Triumphal Arch).

16

The Battle of Britain

When Britain showed no sign of asking for peace, Hitler ordered an invasion plan to be drawn up – *Operation Sealion*. But it was first necessary to gain command of the air over the English Channel.

The Luftwaffe (the German air force) began the attack. British aircraft production, however, was increasing rapidly. Britain also had an efficient radar system which could give advance warning of air attack. And Sir Hugh Dowding – the head of Fighter Command – was a more effective leader than the German air commander Hermann Göring.

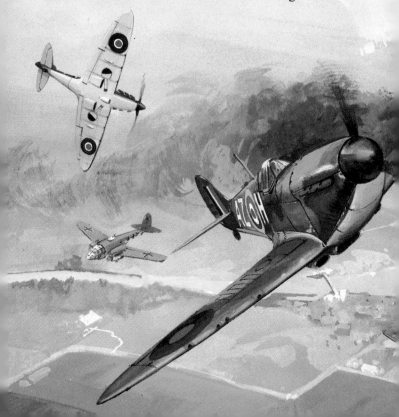

The Battle of Britain began in July 1940. The pilots on both sides were brave and skilful, but the Germans were operating over enemy territory, and their rate of aircraft losses was soon double that of the British. The Royal Air Force was seriously short of trained pilots, but even when their planes were shot down many of them parachuted to safety.

By September the Luftwaffe had shifted its target from the airfields to London and the main cities. Great damage was done. The centres of many English cities were reduced to rubble, but Göring had failed in his main task – to destroy the RAF. *Operation Sealion* was cancelled.

British Spitfires attack a German Messerschmitt fighter before turning their attention to the Heinkel bombers below.

19

Uniforms and Weapons

Most armies went to war in a modernized version of their 1914–1918 uniforms. Camouflage was now universal, from British khaki to German field grey. As the war went on, uniforms tended to become less formal and more practical. In the North Africa campaign soldiers abandoned parade-ground uniforms. Indian soldiers, for example, might wear knitted pullovers. Elsewhere, formal battledress was gradually replaced by camouflage smocks.

British infantryman

German Field Marshal

French legionnaire

Italian infantryman

Russian infantryman

Canadian major

US paratroop officer

Australian infantryman

Indian infantryman

Japanese general

West African rifleman

The infantry rifle and the medium machine-gun had evolved little since World War I, but most armies developed light sub-machine-guns. The Allies used the Thompson and Sten sub-machine-guns. The Germans were equipped with Schmeisser machine pistols (equivalent to sub-machine-guns).

Tanks were key weapons in land warfare. A number of portable anti-tank rocket launchers were developed, such as the British Piat and the American bazooka. The German 88mm anti-aircraft gun also turned out to be a fine anti-tank weapon. Later on it was mounted on tractors and even on tanks. The British equivalent was the 25-pounder field-gun.

British Lee Enfield rifle

German Schmeisser machine pistol

British Bren light machine-gun

German Mauser pistol

British Vickers medium machine-gun

German 6-barrelled Nebelwerfer rocket launcher ('Moaning Minnie')

German 88mm anti-aircraft gun mounted on a tank chassis

Allied (Swedish-designed) 40mm Bofors anti-aircraft gun

23

British PIAT (Projectile Infantry Anti-Tank) rocket launcher

The War at Sea

At the end of World War I the ships of the German High Seas Fleet had been scuttled (deliberately sunk) by their own crews at the British anchorage of Scapa Flow. The British navy had also shrunk during the inter-war years. Even so, Britain entered the war with a more powerful fleet than Germany.

When war broke out the Royal Navy began a blockade of German ports in order to cut off German imports of war materials. The Germans replied by laying minefields. They achieved some successes with a new type of magnetic mine. German U-boats (submarines) also gained important early successes. In October 1939 a U-boat sank the British battleship *Royal Oak* at anchor at Scapa Flow.

In the early part of the war Germany used her surface ships to attack merchant vessels crossing the Atlantic. The merchantmen carried vital supplies from Canada and the United States to Britain.

In December 1939 the 'pocket battleship' *Graf Spee* was cornered by a British squadron in the South

The Graf Spee blows up, scuttled by her own crew. This victory gave new heart to the British people.

Atlantic. After badly damaging the heavy cruiser *Exeter*, the *Graf Spee* withdrew to Montevideo harbour, in Uruguay. Believing that a much stronger British force lay in wait for him, Captain Langsdorff blew up and scuttled the *Graf Spee*. This episode, known as the Battle of the River Plate, did much to restore British confidence after her military defeats.

Both sides, however, had yet to learn how vulnerable surface ships were to aircraft attack. The big ships needed to be protected by escorts of fighter planes. Command of the sea depended on command of the air.

The Battle for the Mediterranean

After the defeat of France the British government became alarmed about the prospect of the powerful French fleet falling into enemy hands. Eventually most of the French ships were put out of action in one way or another. In one incident in North Africa the British ships turned their guns on their former allies; an elderly French battleship, the *Bretagne*, was sunk with great loss of life.

The entry of Italy into the war on the German side intensified the struggle for control of the Mediterranean. In November 1940 British torpedo bomber aircraft sank three Italian battleships in Taranto harbour. This achievement tilted the balance of sea power in favour of the British.

The Italians took their revenge on Christmas Eve 1941. In a daring raid, Italian frogmen badly damaged two British battleships in Alexandria.

A British Swordfish bomber lets go its torpedo at Taranto. These slow, old-fashioned aircraft were nicknamed 'stringbags'.

The Breakout of the Battleships

In November 1940 the pocket battleship *Admiral Scheer* broke through the blockade. By the time she returned to Germany she had sunk 16 merchant ships. The battlecruisers *Scharnhorst* and *Gneisnau* sank or captured 22 more ships before returning to Brest, in France.

In May 1941 the powerful German battleship *Bismarck* succeeded in getting out into the Atlantic. She was engaged by a British squadron. During the ensuing battle the British battlecruiser *Hood* was sunk. The *Bismarck* was finally caught and sunk by gunfire and torpedoes. In the following year the *Scharnhorst*, the *Gneisnau* and the *Prinz Eugen* made a daring dash through the English Channel to Germany. Soon afterwards the *Gneisnau* was damaged beyond repair by bombing. The *Scharnhorst* was sunk in the Battle of the North Cape in 1943.

The Bismarck fired a salvo at the Hood, which quickly blew up and sank. Of the Hood's 1419 men, only three survived.

The Battle of the Atlantic

As the war dragged on it became clear that the U-boats were much more successful than the German surface ships in destroying Allied merchant shipping. The fall of France gave Germany several Atlantic ports from which the U-boats could slip out to attack merchant convoys. These convoys brought vital supplies of food, oil, weapons and ammunition to Britain. Sinkings of merchant ships rose steadily, and the Germans were building U-boats faster than they could be destroyed. Britain came close to being strangled to death.

A German U-boat surfaces to finish off a crippled tanker with gunfire. The tanker's crew would have had small chance of survival, as the submarine could not stop to pick them up.

The U-boats were even more successful when they began to operate in groups, called 'wolf-packs'. U-boat successes reached a peak in 1942.

Allied anti-submarine weapons included depth-charges, which could be set to explode at a particular depth. Sonar (then called Asdic) was a device used to locate U-boats by means of underwater sound waves. By 1943 the Allies had developed a technique of hunting submarines with a combination of surface ships and aircraft, and within the year they regained the mastery of the Atlantic.

In 1944 most of the U-boats were recalled to guard against the Allied invasion of France, bringing the Battle of the Atlantic to an end. When peace was signed the Germans still had nearly 400 submarines – far more than they had started with.

The Widening War

Italy entered the war on the German side in June 1940. Mussolini wanted an easy victory. He decided to attack Greece. To his surprise, the Greeks pushed back the much larger Italian army.

The Italians also had large armies in their African colonies. These were attacked by a small British force based in Egypt. After a series of victories, the British captured Tobruk in January 1941. They were soon poised to take Tripoli and throw the Italians out of North Africa. Then their advance was stopped: 50,000 British troops were needed in Greece.

The map shows the thrust of the German attack on Yugoslavia and Greece in April 1941. The need to aid Greece prevented the British from driving the Italians out of North Africa.

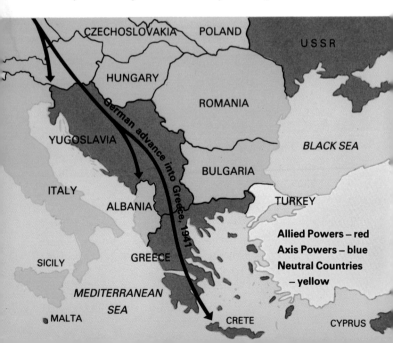

*Paratroops made up the first wave of the German attack on Crete.
The operation was successful, but losses were so heavy that Hitler
never again attempted a large-scale parachute operation.*

Hitler was concerned about the possibility of the
British establishing air bases in Greece. These could
threaten not only Italy but also the important
oilfields in Romania. In April 1941 German troops
invaded Greece and Yugoslavia, overrunning both
countries in three weeks. The British troops were
pulled back to the island of Crete.

German paratroops took Crete in a well-organized
operation the following month. Again, the British
and New Zealand troops had to be taken off. The
evacuation was carried out in great style by the
Royal Navy, despite severe losses from air attack.

The British licked their wounds and wondered
what Hitler would do next. But the evil genius in
Berlin was again looking eastward: on 22 June 1941
Germany invaded Russia.

Operation Barbarossa

Barbarossa was the German code name for the invasion of Russia. The campaign in Yugoslavia and Greece had only held up Hitler's plans by five weeks, but this delay was to prove fatal.

Right up to the invasion Stalin (the Russian dictator) continued to supply Germany with food and war materials. He had always expected Hitler to attack, but even so Stalin seemed to be taken by surprise when the blow fell.

The invasion started well for the Germans, who attacked across a broad front between the Baltic in the north and the Black Sea in the south. Soon the German tanks were only a few hundred kilometres from Moscow. But then Russian resistance stiffened.

German troops advance into Russia during Operation Barbarossa. Hitler expected to defeat the Russians in a matter of weeks.

Russian troops counter-attack outside Leningrad. They were better equipped with warm clothing than the Germans.

Hitler halted the drive on Moscow, and began to attack Russian industrial centres and supply routes.

On the heels of the German army came the dreaded SS 'Action Groups'. Prisoners and Jewish men, women and children were killed, tortured and sent to concentration camps as part of Hitler's 'Final Solution' – the complete extermination of the Jewish race.

Then, in early November, came the fearful Russian winter. The German advance became bogged down, first in mud, then in snow. Hitler had only expected a brief campaign, and many of his troops were not even equipped with winter clothing. *Operation Barbarossa* was not going as smoothly as he had intended.

Pearl Harbor

In the East the Japanese, like the Germans, wished to expand their empire. In 1937 they invaded China; three years later they occupied French Indo-China (now Vietnam). The American, British and Dutch governments promptly cut their trading links with Japan. The Japanese found themselves deprived of vital imports, particularly oil.

On 7 December 1941, without any declaration of war, Japanese aircraft made a surprise attack on the US Pacific Fleet at Pearl Harbor, Hawaii. Eight US

Japanese aircraft attack the battleships of the US Pacific Fleet at Pearl Harbor. The United States was not officially at war, and the battleships were not protected by torpedo nets.

battleships were sunk or badly damaged within half an hour. The next day the United States declared war on Japan and its allies.

Fortunately for the Americans, their aircraft carriers were out at sea on an exercise. The carriers therefore escaped attack. They were to play a vital part in the Pacific War.

Defeat in the Far East

The Japanese were quick to follow up the success of their attack on Pearl Harbor. One after another they captured Allied possessions in South-East Asia.

The main British forces in the area were on the island of Singapore. Two capital ships, the *Prince of Wales* and the *Repulse*, had been sent to reinforce Singapore's defences. Unfortunately they could not be properly protected by aircraft, and three days after Pearl Harbor both ships were sunk by Japanese bombs and torpedoes. This disaster marked the end of the road for the battleship, with aircraft carriers

The map shows the limits of Japanese expansion. The Japanese wished to develop a 'Greater East Asia Co-Prosperity Sphere' – their equivalent to Hitler's ideal of a 'Greater Germany'.

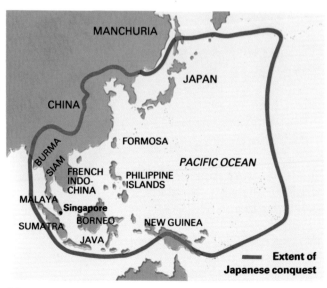

becoming the main factor in sea warfare.

The principal defences of Singapore consisted of big guns pointing out to sea to guard against a naval attack. It was not considered possible for a modern army to attack through the jungles of Malaya. But this is just what the Japanese did, and Singapore was captured on 15 February 1942. It was the largest British army ever to surrender. The British defeat was partly due to poor leadership, but also to the absence of tanks and a severe shortage of aircraft.

Two weeks later a fleet of British, Australian, American and Dutch warships was almost completely wiped out in the Battle of the Java Sea. Only four US destroyers managed to escape.

In April the Japanese cut the Burma Road, which brought vital supplies to China, and by May they had pushed the British back into India.

Japanese troops advance through the Malayan jungle on their way to attack the British naval base at Singapore.

The Turn of the Tide

The fall of Singapore in February 1942 marked the lowest point of Britain's fortunes. On the other hand, *Operation Barbarossa* had swallowed up the bulk of Hitler's armed forces, and Britain was now in much less danger of invasion.

The British now began to increase the scale of their bombing raids on Germany. Civilians on both sides were in far greater danger than in most previous wars. Many people, particularly children, were evacuated from the cities to the countryside. Goods, especially food, were rationed in both Britain and Germany.

An air raid warden issues gas masks to civilians in London. The authorities took what precautions they could to lessen the havoc caused by the bombing of cities.

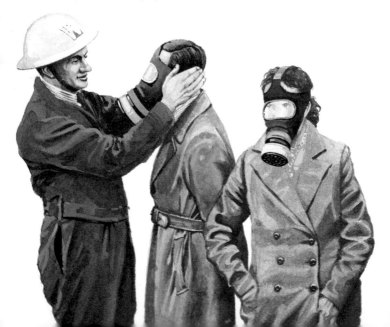

The map shows the limits of German expansion (blue). The Germans were defeated by the vast distances, harsh winters, and limitless manpower of Russia, just as Napoleon had been in 1812.

The problems of the British and German civilian populations were, however, as nothing compared with the sufferings of the peoples whose countries had been seized by the Nazis. Jews, Gypsies, and other so-called 'undesirables' were sent to concentration camps, where millions of them were murdered. The conditions in these camps were so frightful that many ordinary Germans refused to believe the stories they heard.

The SS, which was separate from the main German army, also hired out prisoners to farms and factories as slave labour. Throughout the war the SS made a profit from selling slave labour and stealing prisoners' gold, jewellery and other possessions.

39

The Desert War

The British had halted their advance on the Italian positions in North Africa in order to send troops to Greece; they were to pay a heavy price for this decision. Hitler now decided to reinforce the Italians with a German division under General Erwin Rommel. Rommel struck in February 1941, and the British quickly lost much of the territory they had taken from the Italians. In the meantime, however, Italian ships taking supplies to North Africa were being attacked by British submarines and aircraft from bases on the Mediterranean island of Malta.

When Rommel captured the port of Tobruk in June 1942, the British were pushed back into Egypt. Churchill now decided on a change of command.

General Bernard Montgomery was placed in command of the British Eighth Army. He built up his

supplies and soon had twice as many tanks as his opponents. On 23 October 1942 Montgomery attacked at El Alamein. By early November most of Rommel's tanks had been destroyed, and he was forced to retreat.

Meanwhile, a US army under General Eisenhower landed in French North Africa. The aim was to trap Rommel between the two Allied armies. Rommel fought back with skill and courage. He was, however, constantly hampered by political interference and shortage of supplies. In January 1943 the Allies entered Tripoli. Tunis fell in May, and soon afterwards most of the Axis forces in North Africa surrendered.

The Battle of El Alamein was fought by two of the greatest generals of the war, Montgomery (left) and Rommel (right).

The Battle for Italy

In January 1943, at Casablanca in Morocco, Churchill and President Roosevelt decided on their next move. This was the invasion of the island of Sicily. (They also fixed a date for the invasion of France the following year.) When the Allies landed in Sicily on 10 July they were opposed by German and Italian troops, but within a month the island was in Allied hands. Most of the Axis troops, however, managed to cross the Straits of Messina to mainland Italy.

Meanwhile, Mussolini had fallen from power. He was imprisoned by the new Italian government which lost no time in signing an armistice with the Allies. Allied troops landed on the Italian mainland that very day, unopposed.

US troops emerge from their LSTs ('Landing Ships, Tank') during the Allied landings in Sicily.

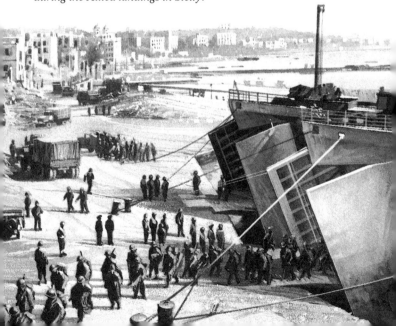

French troops enter Siena during their advance on Florence in 1944. Allied progress through Italy was painfully slow.

The Germans, who had expected the Italians to surrender, continued to fight. When the Fifth US Army landed at Salerno, near Naples, they encountered fierce German opposition, and only just managed to hold on to their position.

The German army was slowly pushed northwards through Italy. The Allied advance was held up for a time by a determined German stand at the ancient monastery of Monte Cassino. On 4 June 1944 the Americans entered Rome. Two days later the Allies invaded Normandy, and world attention shifted away from Italy.

The fall of Rome did not, however, bring the campaign in Italy to an end. Fighting continued almost to the end of the war in the west.

Russia Takes the Offensive

By December 1941 some German army units had reached as far as the outskirts of Moscow, the Russian capital. But now Stalin flung in his reserves for a counter-attack. This was not as successful as Stalin had hoped, but at least it stopped the German advance.

Hitler now took personal command of his forces in the east. His headquarters – the 'Wolf's Lair' – was deep in the forests of East Prussia. In the summer of 1942 the German armies advanced on the Russian city of Stalingrad. This city, largely because of its name, became the scene of a great trial of strength between the two dictators. German troops managed to penetrate the suburbs. The Russians meanwhile grouped factory workers into fighting units.

Opposite: The German army in Russia began to run short of supplies, particularly petrol. Many tanks had to be abandoned through lack of fuel.

Left: Joseph Stalin was the Russian leader during World War II. He was partly responsible for the poor performance of the Russian army at the start of the German invasion. In his pre-war 'purges' he had shot or exiled many of the Red Army officers. However, Stalin soon became a symbol of Russian resistance and refusal to admit defeat.

When the German forces entered Stalingrad, bitter house-to-house fighting followed. But the Germans were running short of vital equipment. The Russians counter-attacked in November, and the German Sixth Army, under von Paulus, was surrounded. The German army still used many horses for transport; by Christmas Paulus's starving men had to eat them. On 31 January 1943 the Sixth Army surrendered.

Both sides now began to build up their forces. A race to build more tanks led up to the greatest tank battle in history, which ended in a Russian victory at Kursk in July 1943. From now on the Russians steadily increased the pressure on the Germans, forcing them on to the defensive.

The War in the Pacific

In May 1942 Japanese forces were threatening both the US base of Hawaii, and the mainland of Australia. The Japanese navy was checked at the inconclusive Battle of the Coral Sea, at which the Americans lost the carrier *Lexington*.

In June the Japanese were heavily defeated at the naval battle of Midway, losing four fleet carriers with their aircraft. Nothing daunted, Japanese troops continued to advance overland in New Guinea and the Solomon Islands. But then US marines landed on the Solomon island of Guadalcanal, in August, and after several months of heavy fighting the Japanese were forced to evacuate their troops.

The Americans went on to retake island after island, simply bypassing some because their supply lines had been cut and they no longer posed a threat.

General Douglas MacArthur led one prong of the American advance on Japan. His troops fought their way through New Guinea to the Philippines. The other prong consisted of the US fleet. The Americans took the Marianas Islands in the summer of 1944. This gave them a shore base from which to bomb the Japanese mainland.

In October 1944 the Japanese lost four more carriers and three battleships at Leyte Gulf. They now began to use a new weapon – *kamikaze* (suicide planes). These were old aircraft packed with explosives and flown straight at US ships. But even this desperate measure was not enough to save Japan from its fate.

Right: A Japanese carrier comes under attack from US aircraft at the decisive Battle of Midway.

Burma – the 'Forgotten Army'

In early 1942 the British army in Burma was in full retreat from the Japanese. India – still a British possession – was now under threat. China was still fighting Japan, but she depended on American support to continue the war, and the only available land route to China was the Burma Road.

The Japanese finally cut the Burma Road at the end of April, and within a month virtually the whole of Burma was in Japanese hands. Nevertheless the Americans continued to supply China by air across the Himalayas – nicknamed the 'Hump'.

Driven back into India, the Allied armies gradually rebuilt their strength. In the end their superiority in the air made the reconquest of Burma possible.

General William Slim

General Joseph Stilwell

Although the Japanese actually advanced into India in March 1944, they were held at bay by the stubborn defenders of Imphal and Kohima. At last, after suffering severe losses, the Japanese were pushed back by superior Allied numbers. Finally, in May 1945, the British retook the Burmese capital Rangoon.

Chiang Kai-shek

Top Left: General Slim, commander of the British troops in Burma. Top right: General 'Vinegar Joe' Stilwell, US commander of the Chinese troops in Burma. Above: The Chinese Generalissimo Chiang Kai-shek. The US kept China in the war by ferrying supplies through Burma.

Left: Allied troops cross a Burmese river. Inset: A location map of Burma.

49

The Final Phase

Late in 1943 the Allied leaders met at Teheran, in Persia (now Iran). Churchill wanted greater US support in Italy. Also, he did not trust Stalin's intentions in eastern Europe, and therefore wished to link up with the Russians in the east. The US president, Franklin D. Roosevelt, insisted that the invasion of Europe should take place in France. From a military point of view this was probably the correct decision but it was to place eastern Europe under communist control.

Meanwhile, the Allied bombing of Germany was increasing all the time. The first 'thousand bomber raid' took place in March 1942, when over 1000 bombers battered Cologne, devastating 600 acres of the city.

Nuremberg was one of many German cities devastated by Allied bombing.

US Boeing Flying Fortresses, protected by a Mustang fighter, on their way to a daylight bombing raid on Germany.

Hamburg was devastated in July 1943 by giant 'block-buster' bombs which caused terrible fires. Britain's Bomber Command used to attack Germany by night. The Americans preferred daylight bombing, which was more accurate but also more dangerous. Large numbers of US Flying Fortress bombers were shot down at first, but losses were reduced when they were provided with Mustang fighter escorts.

Allied bombing became increasingly accurate. The Americans concentrated on destroying factories and fuel production centres, and by the last year of the war Germany was suffering from a severe shortage of fuel. In April 1944, however, there was a lull in the bombing of Germany while the Allies prepared to invade Normandy.

51

The Normandy Landings

General Eisenhower was appointed Allied comman-
der-in-chief for the invasion of France. His German
opposite number was the elderly but able Field
Marshal von Rundsted. Rommel, now Rundsted's
subordinate, worked to improve the coastal defences
with characteristic energy.

The invasion, code-named *Operation Overlord*,
began in rough seas on 6 June 1944. The landing site
was a series of beaches on the coast of Normandy.
Many Allied soldiers were drowned during the landings or killed on the beaches, but the Allies managed
to hold on to their bridgeheads.

*US troops drive inland from their landing beach on the Normandy
coast. Many of the landings were fiercely opposed.*

Partly as a result of Hitler's interference, and partly because of Allied bombing, the German tanks were brought up too late to shake off the invaders. Hitler had by this stage of the war begun to lose his grip on reality.

It took the Allies a month, however, to take the key town of Caen. The breakout from the beaches was also hindered by the thick Norman *bocage* (hedgerows). Allied tanks were only effective after they had been fitted with metal 'tusks' to uproot the hedges in their path.

Once the Allies had taken the port of Cherbourg they could land supplies in increasing quantities. One general at Hitler's headquarters asked Rundsted, 'What shall we do?' 'Make peace you fools', retorted Rundsted. 'What else can you do?' Hitler immediately sacked him.

The July Plot

Von Rundsted was not the only senior officer who was now convinced that the war was lost. The only way for them to prevent the destruction of Germany was to remove Hitler. On 20 July 1944 Colonel Klaus von Stauffenberg smuggled a bomb into Hitler's 'Wolf's Lair' headquarters. The bomb blew out the walls of the wooden building but failed to kill Hitler, who escaped almost unhurt. Hitler's revenge was swift and terrible. Several officers were hanged slowly. Rommel, who had known of the plot, was forced to commit suicide.

Hitler after the explosion. His right arm was stiff and he was slightly burned but otherwise unhurt.

Hitler's Secret Weapons

V1

On 12 June 1944, soon after the Normandy landings, Hitler began to bombard London with V1 flying bombs. Many of the launching sites, however, were bombed or captured.

The V2 rocket was guided by an automatic pilot, and carried nearly a tonne of high explosive. It was the forerunner of modern space rockets.

V2

In August 1944 the Allies succeeded in breaking through the German defences in Normandy. From now on they made rapid progress through France. Paris was liberated on 25 August.

Hitler now began to rely increasingly on his 'secret weapons'. The V1 was a pilotless flying bomb which was used against England. The British managed to intercept many of these 'doodlebugs' with fighter planes and anti-aircraft fire.

The V2 rockets were more deadly. About 2000 of them fell on England. With a top speed of nearly 6000 km/h, they could not be intercepted. Instead, the Allies successfully bombed V2 launching sites.

Members of the British First Airborne Division land near Arnhem by parachute and troop-carrying glider.

Operation Market Garden

By September 1944 the British (under Montgomery) were pushing north-east. Their goal was the Netherlands and the German industrial centre of the Ruhr. Meanwhile the Americans were driving eastwards, towards the heart of Germany.

Operation Market Garden was a plan to drop paratroops behind the German lines and seize the key Dutch bridges. The British, landing at Arnhem, ran into an SS panzer (tank) division. They were badly cut up. Although 2000 troops broke out, most of the rest were captured.

At this point the Allies paused and waited for their supplies to catch up with them, but this also gave the Germans time to strengthen their defences.

The Battle of the Bulge

By the end of 1944 the Allies did not believe Germany capable of launching any further big offensives. They were proved wrong. On 16 December three German armies attacked the Americans in the Ardennes. Two of the German armies were held, but the Fifth Panzer Army (under General Hasso von Manteuffel) created a huge bulge in the American line. The Belgian town of Bastogne was surrounded, but when the American commander was called on to surrender, he replied in one word – 'Nuts'.

Manteuffel's attack ground to a halt when his tanks literally ran out of fuel. German losses were heavy. Hitler's last gamble had failed.

A German tank rumbles past a column of American prisoners on its way to the front during the Battle of the Bulge.

The Drive to Berlin

To the Russians the year 1944 was 'The Year of the Ten Victories'. They began their drive towards Poland in June, and the following month the Poles in Warsaw rebelled against their German conquerors. The SS put down the rebellion with bestial cruelty. The Russians entered the ruins of Warsaw in January 1945. Their determination to fight to the finish was increased by the evidence of German atrocities.

By February the Russians were closing in on Berlin. They were briefly halted by a German counter-attack. On 13 April the Russians took Vienna; on the 16th they renewed their advance on Berlin, and by the 25th Berlin was completely surrounded.

By March 1945 the Allied armies in the west had reached the Rhine. Here they had a stroke of luck. American troops managed to cross the bridge at

Remagen before the Germans blew it up. The race for Berlin – between the British and Americans in the west, and the Russians in the east – was now on. Roosevelt died suddenly on 12 April, but his death brought no slackening of the attack as Hitler hoped it might. Roosevelt was succeeded by Harry S. Truman.

On 30 April, with the Russians only a few hundred metres away, Hitler shot himself. On 2 May British, American and Russian troops linked up on the shores of the Baltic Sea. On 4 May, German representatives signed a surrender document at Montgomery's headquarters. A second ceremony at Rheims, in France, on 7 May 1945, formally ended the war in Europe.

Russian soldiers raise the Red Flag of the Soviet Union over the ruins of the German parliament building in Berlin.

The Defeat of Japan

In early 1945 American forces invaded the two key Pacific islands of Iwo Jima and Okinawa. Okinawa was not taken until June, after desperate Japanese resistance, including thousands of kamikaze attacks on US ships.

On 6 August an American Superfortress bomber dropped an atomic bomb on the city of Hiroshima. The destruction was beyond belief. Three days later a second bomb was dropped on Nagasaki. The Japanese surrendered on 14 August.

The mushroom cloud from the atomic explosion that devastated the Japanese city of Nagasaki on 9 August 1945.

The Aftermath

Churchill (left), Roosevelt (centre) and Stalin(right) met at Yalta in February 1945 to plan the final defeat of Germany.

The victorious Allies divided Germany into four zones. Today, West Germany is made up of the British, French and US zones. The former Russian zone is now East Germany. Poland, Romania, Bulgaria, Czechoslovakia and Hungary have remained under Russian domination ever since the war.

The Nazi leaders were tried for war crimes at Nuremberg. Some were executed, others imprisoned. Six million Jews were murdered by the Nazis and altogether perhaps 30 million people were killed in World War II. This book can only hint at the terrible sufferings of soldiers and civilians alike.

Time Chart

1936 Germany occupies Rhineland

1938 Germany invades Austria

1939
10 March Germany annexes Czechoslovakia
1 September Germany invades Poland
3 September Britain and France declare war on Germany
30 November Outbreak of Russo-Finnish War
13 December Battle of River Plate

1940
9 April Germany invades Denmark and Norway
30 April Japan joins the Axis Powers
10 May Germany invades Belgium, Netherlands and Luxembourg
17 May Germany invades France
26 May Evacuation of troops from Dunkirk begins
10 June Italy declares war on Britain and France
10 July Battle of Britain begins
21 July French sign armistice
28 October Italy invades Greece

1941
6 April Germany invades Yugoslavia and Greece
21 April Greek army surrenders
28 May British army evacuates Crete
22 June Germany invades Russia
1 September Italy invades Egypt
6 December Russians counter-attack at Moscow
7 December Japan attacks US Pacific Fleet at Pearl Harbor
8 December United States declares war on Axis Powers
25 December Fall of Hong Kong

1942
15 February Fall of Singapore
27 February Battle of the Java Sea
4 May Battle of Coral Sea
4 June Battle of Midway
23 October Battle of El Alamein

1943
31 January German Sixth Army surrenders at Stalingrad
1 July United States begins recapture of Pacific islands
10 July Allied landings in Sicily
3 September Italy signs armistice with Allies
9 September American landings at Salerno, Italy

1944
4 June Allies enter Rome
6 June Allied invasion of Normandy begins
20 July Bomb plot fails to kill Hitler
25 August Allies liberate Paris
15 September Arnhem expedition
25 October Japanese navy defeated at Leyte Gulf
16 December Germans launch Ardennes offensive

1945
17 January Russians capture Warsaw
5 February Yalta Conference between Churchill, Roosevelt and Stalin
7 March Allies cross Rhine at Remagen
12 April Death of Roosevelt
28 April Mussolini assassinated
30 April Hitler commits suicide
7 May Final German surrender at Rheims
6 August Americans drop atomic bomb on Hiroshima
9 August Second atomic bomb dropped on Nagasaki
12 September Official Japanese surrender at Singapore ends World War II

Index